Good-byes are too familiar, too unforgiving and
sometimes too hard to say.

OTHER BOOKS BY ROBERT M. DRAKE

Spaceship (2012)

The Great Artist (2012)

Science (2013)

Beautiful Chaos (2014)

Beautiful Chaos 2 (2014)

Black Butterfly (2015)

A Brilliant Madness (2015)

Beautiful and Damned (2016)

Broken Flowers (2016)

Gravity: A Novel (2017)

Star Theory (2017)

Chaos Theory (2017)

Light Theory (2017)

Moon Theory (2017)

Dead Pop Art (2017)

Chasing The Gloom: A Novel (2017)

Moon Matrix (2018)

Seeds of Wrath (2018)

Dawn of Mayhem (2018)

The King is Dead (2018)

What I Say When I'm Not Saying A Damn Thing (2019)

What Happens When I Feel Alone But I'm Not Alone (2019)

What I Feel When I Don't Want to Feel (2019)

What I Really Mean When I Say Good-Bye (2019)

What I Mean When I Say Miss You, Love You & Fuck You (2019)

What I See When My Eyes Are Shut (2019)

For Excerpts and Updates please follow:

Instagram.com/rmdrk
Facebook.com/rmdrk
Twitter.com/rmdrk

ISBN: 978-1-7326900-7-3

Book Cover: Robert M. Drake

For Sevyn & Summer

What I Really Mean When I Say Good-Bye

ROBERT M. DRAKE

BY THE DOOR

The space between us
is beautiful.

You're there
and I'm here
and we could be together,

if only our egos
didn't stop us
by the door.

SOME WOMEN

I've learned how some women
would take it,

they would break everytime
someone told them
they loved them.

While at times,
other women couldn't stand it,

that is,

if you told them
you loved them,
and lied about it,

then that would be
the end for you.

The thing is,
some women are more
than just women.

Some women are dangerous,
they're warriors,

and they'll *eat
your fucking heart* out

the moment you tried
to ruin theirs.

I DO NOT KNOW

I've run out of things
to tell you.

I've run out of feelings,
ideas and heart.

I do not know
what the future holds.

I do not know
if we will be together.

All I know is,
now
and I don't want to stress
over the future
or live in the past…

because this is how it is.

This is how it should be.

Love now
and forget about the rest
right?

But this I tell you,
don't fall for me

goddamn it,
just don't.

I know you're infatuated
with my past,
and I know you want to be
in my future,

but don't.

This is not a good idea,
and I know how things like this
end, and they don't
end well.

Understand,
that I'm no good to you,
that I'm no good
to myself.

Hell, what am I saying.

The wolves have taken over.
My sanity is beyond
the grave
and the madness keeps pulling
at my hair.

The truth hurts,
as all things
people fall in love with

hurt.

And the thing is,
the steady reality
of it all is,

that I've been waiting
several years for someone like you
and now
I have nothing left to give.

I have run out of pieces to break.
I don't have enough for you.

So please,
just go,
there's nothing here left
to give.

SHE GOES

She goes
and sometimes far enough…

and I can't help
but to wonder,

how sometimes,
women like her

show you
how much they love you
with how far

they are willing
to walk away.

TYPEWRITER

I'm sorry
I don't love my typewriter
anymore.

I don't love
the machine.

The ink.
I don't love
the clunkyness,
the way the keys trap themselves
with each press.

I'm sorry
I don't love my typewriter
anymore.

We had a good run,
about seven years
of sorrow and happiness
and anger and love.

We shared too much together
and believed
we would be forever.

I'm sorry
I don't love my typewriter

anymore.

I've moved on,
I've outgrown it.

We no longer see
eye to eye.

I'm sorry
I don't love my typewriter
anymore.

There's so much more
than social media,
than posting excerpts
and killing myself over reviews.

I'm sorry
I don't love my typewriter
anymore.

I just don't.

I love the emotion,
the feeling,
the connection between my words
and other people.

I love what they hate
and I hate only one thing,
that I do not love

my typewriter
as I once did.

Damn.

I've moved on.

Damn.

I cannot finish this poem.
I can't stand it anymore.

Da…

WHAT THEY LOVE

The more people
I loved
the more I understood,

how sometimes
the greatest thing a person
could do is,

let the people say
what they feel

and let them become
what they love.

GETTING ALONG

I love seeing people
getting along.

I love believing
that maybe somewhere,
in some place,
two people
could look each other
in the eyes
without hatred eating away
at their hearts

and say,

"You're my friend."

The reward of peace
is beautiful,

and the reward
of true friendship
is even greater.

UNTITLED

I bought a Ruger
and I think
I did it
to exercise my right
to bear arms.

I don't know why
or when
or how
but I do know one thing.

One day,
the Ruger will come for me
it will weep for company

and when it does
I will be ready.

I will be calm…
and the world
will lose its lights

and I,

will be there.

AFTER OTHERS

Sometimes they want you
and sometimes they don't.

The same way
somethings last
while others don't.

I guess,
what I'm trying to say is,
you don't have to chase people,

that is,

if they don't want you to.

If it's meant to be
then it will happen,
if not,
then you have a lot to realize,

and a lot to lose.

You should only chase people
who know
what running after others
is like.

THIS IS THE PART

This is the part
where you tell me
you love me
and leave.

This is the part
you give me a piece
of yourself
to take it away.

This is the part
you make me feel free
to trap me
in my own cage.

This is the part
I run toward you
so you could walk away.

I guess you could say,
some nights

I fall
into what's not really
there.

TO DO BOTH

You have to love yourself
before loving another person.

You have to have
enough courage
to save yourself,
fight for yourself
and find yourself,

before risking everything
at the price of true love.

And believe me,
the courage it takes
to love another person.

The courage it takes
to love yourself.

The courage it takes
to do both,

day in and day out.

Imagine that.

Now imagine losing everything
but still being lucky enough

to be alive.

The courage it takes
to face the world alone.

The courage it takes
to rise

and start all over
again.

NO ONE IS HERE

You have got to
let people grow
on their own

because sometimes

people get lost
the moment
they are found.

RAIN GIRL

Sad girl,
I see that your eyes
keep raining.

That your soul
keeps breaking,
and that your heart
keeps aching
for more.

Sad girl,
I see the flame of old love
on the edge of your eye.

The hurt
of past lives
and the lonely hour
of your memory.

Sad girl,
I know many things
bring you pain.

I know many things
fall and many things
never learn
how to fly.

Sad girl,
do not lose hope…

please believe
that there are
a thousand beautiful things
waiting for you.

Sunshine comes
to *all* who feel rain.

YOU WIN, SOMETIMES

Understand,
that every second
is a miracle.

Understand,
how there will never be
anyone like you.

Understand,
that true love
does exist.

Understand,
that you will not
understand everything.

Understand,
that sometimes things
won't go your way.

Understand,
that losing someone
isn't always a bad thing.

Understand,
how growing up
never ends.

Understand,
that life isn't perfect
but enough to feel perfect.

Understand,
that you, at times,
will contradict yourself.

Understand,
that sometimes you'll win
but that someone
always
has to lose.

Understand all of these things
and I swear to you,

the love of the gods
will cover you
and it will never leave you astray.

Understand,
that all things divine
live and die

within you.

HEALS ALL

They say time heals
all wounds

and then

there's death,
and for you...

I'd die a million times
to relive

all the things
you once

made me feel.

STEP OUT

Step out of your flesh,
leave the calm of your ocean
and never return.

But do this
not for who you are
but for
who you will become.

Do this
not for the things
you love
but for the things
that hurt.

Do this
not for what brings you peace
but for what disrupts
the heart.

Do this
not for what you know
but for the unknowns
that await you
on the other side.

Do this
not for people,

but for memories,
for glory.

Do this
not to show the world
that you are worthy
of being remembered
but to show yourself
you can do anything
you put your mind to.

Step out of yourself
to find yourself.

Do it.

Do it now.

Before the world
tells you who you are...

and before...

you lose track
of whom you want to
become.

THE BEST THINGS

This life,
for all that it is,
it is all
about perception.

It is all
about what you make it
and how you make it,

for what it is.

By that I mean,
how sometimes,
the best things in life
don't necessarily mean

they are the best things
for everyone.

Sometimes the worse things
can be the best things

and sometimes

the best things
can mean nothing
at all.

SEVEN BILLION

There are seven billion faces,
and at a certain point
of their lives
they will each look
for something.

Most search
for the same thing:

love, sex, money,
fame, etc.

In this great journey,
in this search,
most will find hatred,
racism, and discrimination.

They will run
into a burning wall.

And it doesn't matter
how long they've been searching.

Somewhere down the line
these terrible things
will find them,
to stop them from what it is
they are seeking,

from what it is *you're seeking.*

And these people
will feel pain.
They will tear
and sweat
and walk in fear.

They will struggle
and continue to endure
during this great search.

Eventually,
these special people
do find
what they are looking for.

And they will seem
as if
they have fulfilled their lives.

They will talk about their glory
and drift into the night
in holy laughter.

And as the sun rises
a new day is given,
new breath is given
and revelations are born.

These people,

these seven billion faces
do what they think
is good for them,

and waste their lives
chasing it.

To only discover
that when they find
what they are seeking,

their lives have walked
right by them
and they are left distorted,
lost

in their own void.

Find your own truth
and no one else's.

AMEN.

KEEP GOING

I've always had
this feeling
that you were no good
for me.

I've always felt it
in the middle of my bones
but nonetheless,

I want to thank you
for giving my heart
a chance to move on.

For sometimes
you're forced into the
darkest of places
and sometimes

those same people
give you no choice
but to keep going.

BECOMING ICE

They say,
that I have become cold,
hard and unbreakable.

I say,
that I have become
all of those things
because I have finally learned
how to look out
for myself,
care for myself.

I love me
before I love you.

Now I know
that sounds selfish
but it is true.

So yes,
maybe I am cold,
hard and unbreakable.

Yes, fucker,
I am the goddamn snow blizzard
you wish
you could outrun,

and I'm coming
like a bullet.

So whether you move
or stand,
or hold your breath
or let go…

to choose
to live or die

is completely
up to you.

BORN INTO...

When a baby is born.

When a person saves
someone from death.

When a forest is born
from one tree.

When people find themselves
after years of searching.

When two people feel love
for the very first time.

When someone isn't near
but they seem
closer than ever.

When it rains.
When you kiss.

Every time
you take breath.

When you feel alone
and someone thinks of you.

When a revelation answers

your prayers.

When you tell someone
you miss them
and they feel the same way.

Miracles come
in all shapes and sizes.

All you have to do
is pay attention.

A miracle
is always

waiting to happen.

RELIGION

I know nothing
of religion
and yet,
I speak of miracles
as if
I've met god.

I know nothing
of prayer
and yet,
I've been given a mind
and a pen
and the power
to love.

I know nothing
of people
and yet,
they all feel connected
to the words
that appear
across my heart.

I know nothing
of nothing
but I feel
what I have to feel
to make others

feel something.

I know nothing else
but this.

Maybe god does have a way
of communicating with others.

And maybe
I am nothing more
but his pen,
his words,
thoughts and feelings.

You're not alone.

You never have been
and you never will be.

There is a god
always looking out for you

and always willing
to listen
to what hurts you.

NO MATTER

No matter who you know,
who you love
or what you do.

Do not cage
your heart
for other people.

You must understand
that your soul
is a star

and it needs
its own space
to breathe.

GIVEN TIME

You've got to keep
the kind of people
that make you feel
as if

you could achieve
the impossible...

at any given time.

NOW NOW NOW

Now that we have lost,
felt pain and cried.

Now that we have tasted
the violent, bitter flavor
of death.

Now that we have
seen too much
and lived even more.

Now that we have
gone far enough,
to stand over the edge
of change.

Now that we have
forgotten what worries us,
moves us and makes us
who we are.

Now,
when there is nothing left
to do…

let us all
remember one thing…
to love, heal and grow.

Let us all
arrive in a place
where hands seek
other hands

and eyes
seek other eyes
and hearts
seek other hearts,

to remind themselves
of why we should love

others

the same.

WHAT MATTERS MOST

Sometimes,
the only things that matter
are lost
and very few times

do those same things
return to their
rightful owners.

That's why
when you have something special,
something worth it,
you care for it.

You don't let the things
that make your heart skip
slip away.

GET TOO CLOSE

You've got to
let people get close.

You've got to
let them be there for you
no matter how isolated
you feel.

You've got to
let them help you
and support
what you stand for.

Let them in,
for some people are genuinely
good people.

That some doors
are meant to be left open
and not broken down
by the seeker.

Listen to them,
get to know them
and understand
how you receive
what you put out.
Understand that solitude

can be beautiful
but it can also be
destructive.

Understand
that yes,
some people can empty you
but also,
some people
can save you
from the hollowness
of your soul.

Understand
that not everyone
is out to ruin you,

that some people
really want to see
your magnificent glory
in all colors.

Let these people in,
they're everywhere.

Let them eat with you,
sleep, breathe and live
by you side.

Let them cry,
pray and love.

Let them in.

let them come through
the door without knocking
and without

you asking
who's there.

God bless.

GOES ON

You need to believe
in the power of friendship
and the significance
of strength in numbers.

And remember,
it's your role
to love as many people
as you can

and never forget
how people

can either break
or get stronger
as time goes on.

SHE CRIED

And she cried
as if falling apart
was a beautiful thing
to do.

But in the end,
I didn't want to see her broken,

I didn't want to see her sad
and full of tears.

I wanted her to ride her life
off the rails,

to fall off the edge
of the moon
and land
head first into the sun.

If it only led her
to crash

toward the inspiration
she was meant
to have.

DISCOVER TIME

Together we fall
beneath the black sky
and exchange
all the things we feel.

We say
we love each other
more than anything
else

and for some reason,

I cannot help
but to feel,

like I'm just
discovering something
that's been around

for a very
long time.

RULES AND LAWS

People need rules,
routines,
something to tell them
what to do.

I mean,
take a look at our lives.

We wake up,
go to work,
make someone else money
and then
we go home
to wake up
and do the same thing
the next day.

And some will say
that this is life,

that this is
the way it's supposed to be
but I think they're wrong.

I think there's more
to live for.

For example,

you take a wild bird
and cage it
and it might die

and then
you take a caged bird
and free it
and it will soar beyond
what the eyes could see,

and it's the same way
with people.

You give them the freedom
they deserve
and they will be inspired
to do even more.

They will break the rules
and make the world
a better place.

I know it
and so should you.

WE COULD HAVE

Sometimes I think about you,
and I wonder
why we never gave
each other a chance.

Maybe it was me
or you
or the distance between us
but I know
if you were here
things would be different.

Maybe you and I
could have been something.

Maybe we could have
been happy

and we could have changed
each other's lives.

I THINK OF YOU

I think about you,
and I can't help

but to wonder

if you made it

out alive, if you're okay.

No one is ever really gone.

That's all.

The End.

MISS ME ALWAYS

I hope you will miss me
and think of me.

And I hope you will remember me
for the way I loved you,
for the way I smiled
when I was broken down,
and for the way
I took one last look at you
before I found myself gone.

I hope you will take the time
to look back
and appreciate what we had,
and I hope your heart finds
what it deserves.

I hope you don't feel
the sorrow,
the rain that swallows you whole,

and I hope
isolation doesn't find you.

I hope you don't taste
the bitterness of loneliness
and I hope
you don't find yourself

missing the company
of another person.

This is the type
of burning that never leaves
one's soul.

And I am on fire.

My flesh,
my bones and my soul
are on fire.

Because I was too late.

Too late to realize this...

that sometimes,
the best thing you can do
to someone
is

set them free.

NOT ALL

Not all good-byes
are harsh and hard.

Some good-byes
can be meaningful
and beautiful.

Some can be life changing,
they can make you
or break you.

They can give you
the courage to heal,
to move on,

to forgive and love
yourself fiercely.

The truth is,

you learn a little more
about yourself
every time someone says

good-bye.

RIGHT NOW

Right now
you feel alone
but you should know
that there are still

a lot of good people
out there worth loving.

You just have to
go through several bad ones

to find the ones
worth drowning for.

I AM I AM

I am speaking to you,
writing to you,

to let you know
that you're not alone.

To let you know
that I, too,
feel empty at times,
no matter how many blessings
I've received.

No matter how good it's been.

I don't know what it is
that is meant to fill
this void,
this starved heart.

At times,
I feel like I am spiraling down
this dark well
to only greet the ocean below…

one
I know
I'm not suited for.

I don't have
the strength to swim.

I am exhausted
from trying to figure things out,

from trying to live up to what others
want me to be.

So you're not alone.
You never were.

Not physically,
emotionally or spiritually.

You have people here
with you who care.

People who are willing
to give you
your space when you're trying
to figure out the stars
in your head…

and that's a blessing

whether you know it
or not.

You're never quite alone
no matter how far you go,

and you should never regret
opening up to people
who know
what it's like
to be in your shoes.

NEVER SAY IT

You should never
expect to find
a piece of yourself

in the same place
you felt lost.

The same way
you should never

expect to find love
in the same people

who left you
broken.

POWER IS...

You're not
what they want you to be.

You're not
the labels people put on you,
and you're not
what you fear,
what they fear.

You're not
your past,
although,
you should never forget it.

And you're not
your flaws:

the errors they catch
and the scars that break you
every once in a while.

You're not any of that.
You're so much more,
regardless
of your faults...

because you've got something
most people don't have

and *that's guts,* kid.

You inhale,
take it all in
and never think twice
of their opinions.

That's power.

Your world is made of confidence
and fire,

and the only one
who could destroy it

is you.

BEYOND THIS

You've got to
take everything they say,
good or bad
and carry it
behind your back
like a pair of wings.

You've got to fly,
my love,
find adventure
beyond this city.

You've got to move on,
find yourself
in places you never knew existed.

You've got to meet
new people,
the ones who know
more about you
than yourself.

The ones you never thought
you'd meet.

You've got to find
your perfect freedom,
my love,

expand your arms,
and dominate your life
with no fear.

You've got to believe
that there's still a fight in you.

So take it, my love.
Know it, my love.

Understand that your life
is the most precious thing
in the world
and know

that there is nothing
more beautiful

than experiencing
the love of another person.

DEATH COMES

I must have died
last year
because I can no longer feel.

Now this is when
things get real.

When you feel
like you've been dead all year long,
not being able
to feel.

Not being able
to know what it is
that you're missing.

This is how it sparks.

Like one day,
you're living your life
and loving your life

and then
it hits you
like a ray of light.

It hits you
but not hard enough

to notice the impact.

That is when things change.

When people
begin to move their mouths
but you don't hear the words
being projected.

This is what it's like
to be left alone.

To be loved one day
to only be a burden
the next.

That is what it's like
to walk a thousand miles
and not find your way
back home.

To tell someone
you love them
and not hear it
in return.

The world ends
and all that is left
are the burning memories.

The ones you've aired out

and the ones
you've drowned
in the river of your veins.

This is the void.

The lost space scientist cannot explore.

The new low.
The deepest parts
of your heart.

This is how it ends.

The moment you realize
the person you love
no longer feels the same way.

Your legs are still.
Your arms are still.
Your eyes and face,
still,

and all that is left
is what you carry inside
and it sinks within you
like a weight
piercing through the sheets,
the layers of your soul.

I can no longer feel,

adapt.

I can no longer hurt,
cry.

I've gone beyond those things,
beyond what this
human experience guarantees.

I must have died last year
and now,
I am waiting where the gods await,

where perfection
and sorrow collided.

Where stars go to die
where only the lonely reside.

I am a fool.
Yes,
that I am,
but I am a fool

who has once held love with care,
and now,
like the fool
that I am

I have lost it and I regret
letting it slip away.

SENSES

I have this deep sense
of feeling

that some of me
isn't real,

that some of me
isn't here

and that some of me
isn't meant

to be mended again.

THE LESS YOU...

I sometimes wonder
where all that love you had
for me went.

Did it walk out of your life?

Did you throw it away?

Or did you lose it
one night while you were alone?

And then,
after all this time,
it comes to me.

The less you gave,
the more I found.

The further you went,
the closer I was.

The less you cared,
the more I loved
and because of that
you helped me find myself.

It was one of those things
I didn't know

until now.

So thank you
for everything you never gave me.

For all the love,
attention and time
you didn't have.

I'm stronger now
and I wouldn't be who I am
without that.

This is my metamorphosis
and the change

is out of this world.

MY PAST

I can't change
my past
and I can't understand
my failures.

But I have loved you
with my mind,
body and soul,

and that
has brought me closer
to happiness

than I have ever been.

TEARS, MAN

When the tears are gone
and the gentle ache
the heart brings fades…

you will know
that it was all for something.

Therefore,
you must take this with you.

Place it in a safe place
but do not forget it is there.

Follow your path,
accept your flaws
and hold on to your heart
when things change.

You're welcome,
and watch your step.

UNDO THINGS

You can't undo things,
and you can't
go back to how things were.

What you said
has been done
and what you've done
will never come back
to you
even if you tried.

All you can do
is make peace with what you've lost.
With what you've learned
to accept of yourself.

No matter what has happened,
you're a better person…

no matter how many worlds
you've destroyed.

You're a better person…

no matter how many times
you've had to
put up with yourself
for the mistakes you've made.

The idea of tomorrow
can be a beautiful thing,

if only you let
all that brings you harm

pass you by.

SO MUCH OUT OF ME

You take so much
out of me
but also put
so much back in me.

And that is why
I love you.

I exhale,
you inhale,
and never do I experience
the same breath twice.

You give me life
in all, unforgiving places.

In the water, I am yours.

In the air, I am yours.

In the flames,
and in the places
I have yet to discover.

And never
have I been able
to envision

what my life would be like

without the thought
of you.

THE GROUND FALLS

The ground is solid
and the air is thin.

I fall. I fall. I fall.

And this is what
growing up
must feel like.

Like seeing,
and knowing,

how everything
fucked up can possibly happen
to you beforehand

and still
charge straight toward it
with a smile.

Responsibility is a bitch
and life
is just another metaphor

for pain.

MOST PEOPLE

Most people are exhausted.

They're tired of the horrors
life brings.

Which is why
most
don't want to read
about darkness.

There's too much pain
going around lately,
too much
human suffering.

People want to heal.

They want peace.

They want to be left alone.

They crave something positive,
anything,
to help them
get through their day.

People need light
just as much as they need

darkness.

They need something to
distract them

from the pain they carry
within.

DO NOT

Do not fall in love with me.

I am not easy
to love
and I know
it might be a bad thing

because I know
I demand so much.

I'm not the softest person
and I have
a whole goddamn list
of things
I require.
And none of them
come easy.

Most of them are hard.
Most of them
aren't for the faint hearted.

I have standards
because I know
what I want, what I deserve
and I know
what I have to offer.
I'm a cloudy day,

the soft rain above the sea,
the last breath
from a warm good-bye.

I'm all sadness combined
in one person,

all tears
that fall from tired eyes
and all things
that wrap around a broken heart.

What I am trying to say is

I'm not perfect
and I don't expect you
to be either,

but I know my worth.

And I love
with all tenderness,
carefulness
and with everything I do not know
about myself.

I just want something real.

Someone
who isn't afraid
of what goes on within,

and I demand nothing less
than that.

I know who I am
and I know
how everything ends
and begins with me.

So please,
do not fall in love with me…

I know
you can do so much better
than that.

YOUR HEART

That's who your heart
belongs to.

The last person
you think of
right before
you fall asleep

and the first person
you think of
when you wake.

That's who your heart
belongs to…

take notice of this
and remind them
of how much

you need them
before

they are gone.

NO ONE UNDERSTANDS

No one understands you.

Well,
of course not.

We all feel this way
and to some degree
we don't expect
to be understood,

but we do expect
someone to be there.

Someone
with enough patience
to try,
to break us down
to the very core
of ourselves.

This is what makes
life beautiful.

To have people
try...

and try and try
to be there for you...

to try to save you
even if they know

they cannot.

AND NOW

And now,
when I look into your eyes,
I feel something,
and I don't necessarily know
what it means.

But I do know it stings.
It hurts.

It stirs the waters
from the soul.

And sometimes
it feels as if my life
is being dragged out of my body,
pulled into another realm,
another dimension.

The thing is,
you left a lot of pain in me,
darling.

In my eyes and hands,
and because of it
my fingers are broken.

I'm too fragile.
I can't find love

ROBERT M. DRAKE

in another person.
I can't hold on to another heart.

I don't have it in me, baby.

And now,
since you've been gone,
almost everyone I meet
thinks
they can heal me,
thinks
they have enough in them
to fix me,

to bring me back
to what I once was.

I hate that.

I hate that I've become
a task, a puzzle
wanting to be solved,
and I can't stand it.

I'm broken man,
a mad man
lost in a sea of lost love.

Barely hanging on,

but those eyes of yours...

they make me smile.

They bring out
the innocence in me.

They bring out
these familiar feelings
I think I've felt before.

It's stupid, I know,
but no one ever told me
this is what
it would be like.

No one ever told me
that a woman's eyes
are deeper than all the oceans

and how
even the strongest of men
can drown.

Those eyes
have stripped my flesh
bare to the bone,

and now
there is nothing left of me
to see.

You had me

all this time
while I was out looking for myself.

And now,
I am yours:

mind, body, soul and all.

And like a flower set on fire,

I embrace the flame
as the burning fragrance of defeat
fills the air.

I love you

and sometimes, love
comes to this.

To slow deaths
and slow burnings

and no one in the world
can ever explain

why.

IT BEGINS

And yes,
I have failed
at many things,
but this is not
how it ends.

This is how it begins.

This is how
I shatter
into a million different pieces,
to discover myself
a million different ways.

This is my time,
my awakening,

and I can feel
the universe spinning

on the tip
of my tongue.

BEEN HERE BEFORE

We've been here before,
and we both know
very well how it goes,
how it ends.

And still,
we wonder what it is all for,
what does it all mean
and why do we continue
to do it.

Why do we continue
to put ourselves
through so much pain.

Love and life.

This hurting,
breaking
and the ache it leaves behind.

We know a little
too much of what to expect
from love
and a lot less
of who we are,

to the point

where we are
looking for who we are
in other people's lives,
ideas and expectations.

I want to love you,
I do,
but I know far too much
of how it would affect me,
of how it would bury me
beneath the earth

the moment it all goes
to shit.

And it will
because it always does.

We have this urgency
of finding love,
of giving love
and not knowing
a goddamn thing about love
to begin with.

And then we ask ourselves
why we are crazy,
why we are numb
and empty

because

we've been here before
and yet,

it all feels different every time.

Love and life.
Life and love.

It is all the same.

Chaos and laughter.
Laughter and death.

It is all the same.

People and places.
Places and memory.

It is all the same.

That person in the mirror
and who you dream of being
one day.

It is all the same,

but in all aspects
it makes you real.

So yes,
we've been here before,

you and I.

We know how this is going to end,
and
the beauty of it is,

although
it is not meant to last forever,
we fight hard
for that one moment

that is meant
to take our breaths away.

One love, my sweet people.

Find it,
even if you lose
everything you love.

ALONE IN THE NIGHT

If being alone
has taught me anything,
it has taught me

how to be strong
when needed,

how to let go
when there's nothing left
to hold on to,

and how to value myself

before giving my love
to anyone else.

HERE I STAND

Here I stand,
thinking, wondering,
if anyone
feels what I feel.

If anyone grieves
and hurts the way I hurt.

And so,
it comes to me
as if I am the last person
on the planet.

As if I am the only person
looking at the flowers,
daydreaming
about the beautiful people
I've lost.

As if I am the last one left
with a handful of scars
and a long list of regrets,
buried beneath the last song
I sang.

This pain does not define me
but in all honesty,
who am I?

I ask
as all things that end
haunt my last breaths.

What is this delicate sadness
that fights gently into our hearts?

Tell me what does it all mean?

*Why does it sting
the way it stings?*

Tell me about these fingerprints,
the ones that have made a home
out of my heart.

And tell me why I can still remember
a little of my past.

Am I supposed to let go
or hold on?

Am I supposed to fall on purpose?

Knowing
I am not strong enough to fly?

I ask,
if I am really here.

If all of this darkness

is real,
if any of it
is any good for me.

No one seems to know.

No one seems to even care.

And this is how
my meaning finds its way
into my life.

This is how
and when it all makes sense.

It is in all the moments
I feel lost...
when I am mostly full of self-doubt,
questions
and insecurities

where I find myself.

Where I recognize my smile.
I am an anchor
and I belong in the bottom
of the sea.
And anyone
brave enough to dive toward the bottom
will drown with their eyes closed.
I am more

than what you see

but still,
I am wondering
if anyone feels what I feel.

If anyone has died
the ways I have died

and if anyone
has been brought back
to life

by someone
who understands.

FIGURE IT OUT

You have to
figure things out
on your own.

Life is about timing.

You have to trust
what it gives you

and

make flowers
of all things
that mean you harm.

THE TWO

You have to know
that you are full,

and not half full
or almost full

but completely
from top to bottom.

You have so much
inside of you
and it is enough space

to demand more
than a couple of meteors
and stars.

You have to believe this
and understand

that emptiness
is a state of mind.

That brokenness
doesn't last long enough

and that

the flow of time
moves quicker

than you can realize
the two.

WALK AWAY

And as you walked away,
I slowly touched the void
in your soul.

And as I did,
it filled mine.

And that's what destroyed me.

(Or so I believe.)

The way I finally saw you
for who you were
but by then,

of course,
as all things that
are good to me…

it was
too late.

TIME AND TIME

Don't be so hard on yourself
when you find yourself
dwelling on your past
and overthinking
about all the misfortune
you've had.

Because sometimes
people forget
that their past is a pathway.

And a pathway is a journey.
And a journey takes time.

And time is all you have
when you feel lost.

So please be patient
and kind.

Something better
is on the way.

IT NEVER LEAVES

The emptiness never left.

It now inhabits
a smaller space in me
and sometimes

it makes me feel
like I'm the last person alive.

Empty rooms need to be filled
and empty souls do too.

And sometimes
no matter how decorated
they are…

the two always
find it within their nature

to let
all that is within
slip away.

Time passes,
and almost
always empty spaces
remain empty
all of the time.

BLACK HOLES

You shouldn't fall
because you feel heavy.

You shouldn't break
because you feel so fragile.

And you shouldn't hold on
to the first person
who lets you slip away.

Remember your worth.

This is the year
and the next

you will discover
that you are made of love,

that you are made of black holes
and other broken things.

MADLY, FOOLISHLY IN LOVE

I am madly, foolishly
in love with you…

lost backwards in you
with no escape.

And it feels
like my heart
has been pierced by flowers
instead of knives.

For once, I feel good.

I feel invincible.
I feel like I am walking
between the space
where lighting and thunder merge.

If there has ever been a moment
to live,
it is this one.

In times
when I am with you,
thinking of you,
crying over you
and remembering you.
All meshed into one.

This sweet pain fulfills me.

It gives me hope
in times of darkness.

In times when I have
left it all
on the table.

Alone I drain myself out.

I had a hole
in the middle of my chest
and now it is gone.

Your hand has covered it
and it has given my heart
another chance.

Thank you.

THE MESSAGE

Recreate yourself,
adjust to the times
and how they change,

and don't forget
to plant flowers

in the darkest depths
of your soul.

COLD HEART

She says I'm cold,

that I do not know
how to love.

That even when I'm trying
I still
find a way to fuck things up.

I reminisce
while we're in bed,

and I collect all
that I've been through
on a whim.

I smile at my past
as I attend my wounds
and pull another arrow
from my back.

I gently laugh.
The silence fills the room
and still,

she wonders how many times
I have been shattered.

To have the audacity
to give myself to her

with a missing
heart.

YOUR LIFE

You took your life away.

Riding through airplanes,
lost and confused while
staring out of the window.

It must be hard.
It must be dark.

Confusing, that I know.

It must be lonely up there.

You must be
missing your friends,
family, my brother.

You must be imagining
how it's like without you here.

Wondering
if anyone is missing you.

Wondering
if what you did
was the right thing to do.

No one knows

No one ever will.

No one ever finds
their way…

and I think
most of us
are the same way as you
or close enough.

I can only imagine, my brother.

I can only
close my eyes to be surrounded
by the darkness.

I can only lie on my bed…
to feel
what it was like…

what you felt
when you were
lying in your coffin.

My brother,
will you forgive me?

For that last night
you called
and I did not answer
because it was too late.

It must have been hard.
It must have been dark.

It must have been lonely,
and now the tables
have turned.

And all my life
I have been confused
about life.

All my life
I have been living backwards.

I am sorry, my brother.

I cannot forget your face,
your smile.

I cannot forget how brave
you were.

How strong that heart was.

If I can bring you back
I would… and
if death was a place,
then I would walk across
the world to find it,

to pull you from it

and greet you in breath.

My brother,
I can only imagine.

I can only dream
of what it is like for you
on the other side.

I hope you are okay
and I hope you are
finally free

wherever
you have gone.

MOST TIMES

I feel so much
at times,

that I barely

feel anything
at all.

A PERSON

A person
is just a person

until you feel them,
spend time
with them

and understand them.

And then,
they become more

and before you know it,

it is over

in a blink of an eye.

TWO BIRDS

Well, it's sad isn't it?

The language of love,
the translation of it.

How it begins and how it ends.

Like one day you're together,
losing yourselves
in the hours, talking till 3 a.m.,
sharing secrets the world
has yet to know.

And then,
a flash happens,
and the next moment,
you're just people.

Two ordinary people
who used to know
one another.

Two ordinary people left behind.

Life is funny, you know?

It gives
and it takes

and it has no mercy,
no remorse.

It just does what it has to do,
regardless
if your feelings get hurt
or if you win or lose.

That's life.
That's love.

You just have to trust
your timing.

Trust what's handed
to you
and what's not meant
to be yours.

From people
to moments
to things.

What is yours
will always be yours

and what isn't

will slip through your hands
like hot sand.

THE HARDEST PART

The hardest part
is coming to the realization,

that no one
is really going to save you
but yourself,

that pain
is your life's most valuable teacher

and that

you will never find happiness
until you are

completely,
absurdly

in love
with yourself.

HOW LONG

I wonder how long
you would hold on
to the wrong person

until

you realize
that the only feelings
you should be

worrying about

are that
of your own.

I WONDER

I wonder if people
feel the same as me.

If they feel exiled
from their own skin.

If they feel confused
about being who they are.

And if they go through
their lives believing

they are capable
of so much more.

FLOWERS AND SCARS

I want flowers on my back
instead of scars.

I want books
instead of guns.

And I want peace
instead of war.

I want to live.

I want life
to be my only option.

I want air
to fill my lungs
and I want the smoke
from burning buildings
to fade.

I want love
but not the love
of someone else.

I want self-love.

I want hands to touch hands
and fist

to become fist
if only
to express power,
and not violence.

I want freedom
but not the freedom to go
where you want.

I want liberation of self.

I want
to become who I want
to become
and not be prosecuted
or judged over it.

I want humanity,
connectivity
even if it is only with these words.

I want to feel
without knowing what it is
I feel.

To flourish
in something new,
something undiscovered.

Like the blooming of love,
unconditional love.

That's all I want.

Greatness and connection, forever.
Love and happiness, forever.
Life and blessings, forever.

Forever.

Until the last sun
devours the dirt

and the dust in our bones
return to the stars.

TRUTH

I just want the truth.

The truth about grief,
life, loss and love.

And I don't want it
sugar coated to protect the past.

I don't want the people
I love
to hold back
about what's really going on
in order to protect me.

To save me
from some kind of terrible feeling.

I want the truth,
goddamn it, and I want it
even if it hurts.

Even if it
leads me toward my doom.

I don't want to die
with a handful of lies,
with more questions
than answers,

and I don't want to chase
something that's not there.

I'm sorry
I'm being too demanding,
but I can't help it.

I can't control the urge to know.
To break things
down to the atom and understand them.

So please,
go ahead,
take my soul
and throw it in the fire
but don't tell me
it won't hurt.

Don't tell me
it won't scorch me,
and don't tell me

I'm what you've always
been looking for—to leave
by morning.

Give me what's real,
the nitty gritty of things

because
I'd rather live with the truth

than live the rest of my life

wondering

where it all
went wrong.

ON SADNESS

How sad
it is
to fall in love
with words
instead of actions.

To break over letters
and drown in a body
of water

that doesn't exist.

ESCAPING IT ALL

Some people
get the best of you
and it's not your fault
because some people
are assholes.

That's just how it is
but still,
I admire you for what you do,

knowing how they are,
knowing that some of them
are only in it
for themselves.

And no matter how many times
you've been hurt
you still give people chances

because you believe in change,
in the greater good.

I admire that about you.

You don't know people's true intentions
and still,

you treat everyone

as you'd like to be treated.

I respect people like that,
like you.

People who give
and give and give
until there's nothing left
to give.

You deserve a crown,
a kingdom of flowers
away from the bullshit

and a pair of wings
to fly,

whenever you feel
like escaping
from it all.

SAME PEOPLE SAME MIND

We read the same books,
watch the same movies,
and visit the same places.

And yet,

we are all so different

and on many levels
we are drowning

all the same.

AND YET...

We feel,
we cry,
we crash
and burn.

And yet,
none of us
want to let go
of the things

that weigh us
down.

YESTERDAY

Be better than
yesterday.

Be better than
who you used to be
before this very moment.

And be that person
who looks back

and says:

*"I gave you the best of me
and I am still here."*

Regardless of whom you are
or who

you're meant to be.

SELF-LOVE

Love yourself.

I cannot stress it enough.

Love yourself
if it is the only thing
you do or believe in.

Love yourself,
do it, but do it
because you must,
because there is
no other way to live.

No other way
to love another person.

Love yourself.

Put yourself first,
know that you are
the most important person
in your life.

Love yourself.

Fiercely and bravely,
and I know

it is one of the most
confusing things to do,
hardest things to do
but you must
learn to do so…

if you want a fair shot
at happiness.

Love yourself.

I cannot stress it enough.

Love yourself, goddamn it.

You do not have to be perfect.
You weren't born to be.

You were born to grow
through error.

To love
through heartbreak
and to live
through loss.

This is how you'll learn.
This is how you'll know,
that the greatest tragedy
in life is
believing in all the things

that break you

and not loving yourself
enough

to believe
that you are more.

VIOLENT PEOPLE

Some people
rule through violence
and power.

They must believe
that this is the only way
to move people

but they are wrong.

Fear is no blessing.
Destruction is no light.

Love is the greatest gift,
understanding connects humanity

and *kindness is everything,*

my sweet, people.

I SWEAR, MAN

That's what hurts the most.

The fact that I gave you
almost everything I had.

My time,
heart and art.

And in the end,
I got nothing,
not even a decent good-bye,

just a mouthful
of empty words
that felt
like they were missing something,
words that didn't mean
anything.

But it's all good.

I probably deserved it.
I probably caused it
on my own.

And I probably
wouldn't even be where I am
if it wasn't for you.

So I'm not sure
if I should thank you
or tell you to fuck off.

I'm not sure
if I'm in a good place
or in an even worse place
than before.

I'm not sure
if I should be happy
for having a little bit left,
perhaps even enough
to breathe

or sad
for being alone,
confused…
where the darkness dwells.

These things,
I swear, these people.

The more I give,
the more I lose.
And the more I lose
the less I feel,
the more I lose track
of myself.

And like I said,

that's what hurts
the most.

When I'm with someone I
give them 100% of myself
and it's just sad,

that still,
after all the bullshit people go through,
some people
just don't get it.

Some people take
and take and take
without ever giving back

a piece of themselves.

I swear, man…

some people make me sick.
They want everything
for themselves

but fail to give
in return.

CPSIA information can be obtained
at www.ICGtesting.com
Printed in the USA
FSHW020948220719
60271FS